Festivals in Different Cultures

Ramadan

by Lisa J. Amstutz

raintree

a Capstone company — publishers for children

Raintree is an imprint of Capstone Global Library Limited, a company incorporated in England and Wales having its registered office at 264 Banbury Road, Oxford, OX2 7DY – Registered company number: 6695582

www.raintree.co.uk
myorders@raintree.co.uk

Edited by Jill Kalz
Designed by Julie Peters
Picture research by Pam Mitsakos
Production by Steve Walker

Printed and bound in China

ISBN 978 1 4747 3796 8
20 19 18 17 16
10 9 8 7 6 5 4 3 2 1

British Library Cataloguing in Publication Data
A full catalogue record for this book is available from the British Library.

Acknowledgements
We would like to thank the following for permission to reproduce photographs:
Getty Images: Rich-Joseph Facun, 17; iStockphoto: SoumenNath, 5; Shutterstock: Aisylu Ahmadieva, 11, AmazeinDesign, 15, callmerobin, 1, 22, 24, back cover, clicksahead, cover, Digital Saint, design element, Firas Nashed, 10, JOAT, 3, Kertu, 13, MidoSemsem, 21, Mrs_ya, 9, muratart, 19, rSnapshotPhotos, 6 inset, ZouZou, 7, 14

All the Internet addresses (URLs) given in this book were valid at the time of going to press. However, due to the dynamic nature of the Internet, some addresses may have changed, or sites may have changed or ceased to exist since publication. While the author and publisher regret any inconvenience this may cause readers, no responsibility for any such changes can be accepted by either the author or the publisher.

Contents

What is it?

Be kind to one another.

Ramadan is here!

Ramadan is a Muslim holiday.

It is a time to be good.

It lasts one month.

Time to pray

People do not eat
all day. They do not
drink either.

People pray.

They think about God.

People do kind things.

They help others.

They give food and money.

The sun sets.

People light candles.

They eat dates.

Then they eat a meal.

Time for joy

The month is over.

Families have a feast.

They thank God.

Pop! Boom!

Fireworks fill the sky.

The party lasts three days.

It is a happy time.

Glossary

feast large, fancy meal for a lot of people on a special occasion

kinara candlestick used to hold seven candles at Kwanzaa

symbol something that stands for something else

unity being together as one

Read more

It's Ramadan and Eid Al-Fitr! (It's a Holiday), Richard Sebra (Lerner Classroom, 2016)

My First Ramadan (My First Holiday), Karen Katz (Square Fish, 2015)

Ramadan and Id-ul-Fitr (Holidays and Festivals), Nancy Dickmann (Raintree, 2011)

Websites

www.ramadan.co.uk/kids-corner/
Enjoy activities and games while learning about Ramadan!

www.kiddyhouse.com/Ramadan/
Get answers to all your questions about Ramadan. You can also play games, do crafts and learn songs.

Comprehension questions

1. Name three things people may do during Ramadan.

2. At the end of Ramadan, families have a feast. What is a feast?

Index